EXPLORING THE
AZTEC EMPIRE

by Laura K. Murray

12 STORY LIBRARY

www.12StoryLibrary.com

12-Story Library is an imprint of Bookstaves and Press Room Editions

Produced for 12-Story Library by Red Line Editorial

Photographs ©: Rafal Kubiak/Shutterstock Images, cover, 1, 19, 29; North Wind Picture Archives, 4, 9, 10, 14, 16, 22, 24; Globe Turner/Shutterstock Images, 5; Leon Rafael/Shutterstock Images, 6; Sergey SP/Shutterstock Images, 7; NativeStock/North Wind Picture Archives, 8, 22; Glass and Nature/Shutterstock Images, 12; Noradoa/Shutterstock Images, 13; stockcam/iStockphoto, 15; tateyama/Shutterstock Images, 17; Fabio Imhoff/Shutterstock Images, 18, 20; Arian Zwegers CC2.0, 19, 29; Faviel_Raven/Shutterstock Images, 21; Jesus Cervantes/Shutterstock Images, 23; Nancy Carter/North Wind Picture Archives, 25, 28; Sang Tan/AP Images, 26; Carol M. Highsmith/The Lyda Hill Texas Collection of Photographs in Carol M. Highsmith's America Project/Library of Congress, 27

Content Consultant: Kimberly Gauderman, Associate Professor, Department of History, University of New Mexico

Library of Congress Cataloging-in-Publication Data
Names: Murray, Laura K., 1989- author.
Title: Exploring the Aztec Empire / by Laura K. Murray.
Description: Mankato, MN : 12 Story Library, [2018] | Series: Exploring
  ancient civilizations | Includes bibliographical references and index. |
  Audience: Grades 4-6.
Identifiers: LCCN 2016046442 (print) | LCCN 2016047924 (ebook) | ISBN
  9781632354679 (hardcover : alk. paper) | ISBN 9781632355324 (pbk. : alk.
  paper) | ISBN 9781621435846 (hosted e-bk.)
Subjects: LCSH: Aztecs--Juvenile literature. | Mexico--Civilization--Juvenile
  literature.
Classification: LCC F1219.73 .M87 2018 (print) | LCC F1219.73 (ebook) | DDC
  972--dc23
LC record available at https://lccn.loc.gov/2016046442

Printed in the United States of America
022017

Access free, up-to-date content on this topic plus a full digital version of this book. Scan the QR code on page 31 or use your school's login at 12StoryLibrary.com.

Table of Contents

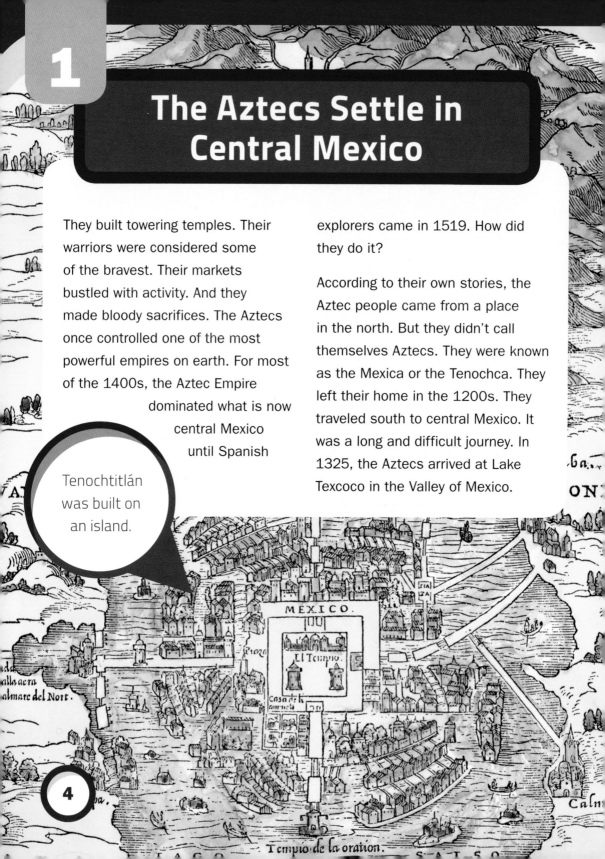

The Aztecs Settle in Central Mexico

They built towering temples. Their warriors were considered some of the bravest. Their markets bustled with activity. And they made bloody sacrifices. The Aztecs once controlled one of the most powerful empires on earth. For most of the 1400s, the Aztec Empire dominated what is now central Mexico until Spanish explorers came in 1519. How did they do it?

According to their own stories, the Aztec people came from a place in the north. But they didn't call themselves Aztecs. They were known as the Mexica or the Tenochca. They left their home in the 1200s. They traveled south to central Mexico. It was a long and difficult journey. In 1325, the Aztecs arrived at Lake Texcoco in the Valley of Mexico.

Tenochtitlán was built on an island.

MEXICO.

Plaza

El Templo.

Casa del

Tempio de la oration.

THE MEXICAN FLAG

You can see Aztec history on the Mexican flag. In the middle of the flag is a picture of an eagle eating a snake. The eagle sits on a cactus on a rock above a lake. This is the sign that told the Aztecs to settle Tenochtitlán on Lake Texcoco.

There they saw an eagle perched on a prickly pear cactus. The eagle was eating a snake. The Aztecs thought eagles were strong and powerful. The Aztecs took this as a sign that they had reached their new home. They founded the city of Tenochtitlán on a small, swampy island. It later became the capital of the Aztec Empire.

Tenochtitlán was a city-state, or *altepetl*. City-states are cities that have their own government. The Valley of Mexico had many city-states. Each had its own leader. In 1428, Tenochtitlán

5 million

Approximate population of the Aztec Empire at its height.

- The Aztec Empire controlled most of central Mexico during the 1400s.
- Tenochtitlán was the capital of the Aztec Empire.
- In 1428, the cities of Tenochtitlán, Tezcoco, and Tlacopan formed the Triple Alliance.

joined with two other city-states, Tezcoco and Tlacopan. The three formed the Triple Alliance. Together they were stronger. The Aztec Empire began its rule.

Mexico's flag

2

The Aztecs' Mighty Army Grew the Empire

After 1428, the Triple Alliance of Tenochtitlán, Tezcoco, and Tlacopan grew quickly. The new empire conquered more than 400 city-states in the Valley of Mexico. It stretched from the Gulf of Mexico to the Pacific Ocean.

Aztec warriors began their training as children. Most warriors were men. But women would fight to protect their homes and families. When called to battle, the Aztec army would fight to take control of the enemy's temple.

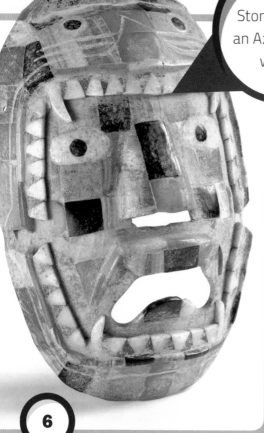

Stone mask of an Aztec jaguar warrior

In battle, warriors used swords with rows of sharp obsidian blades. The warriors also used clubs, slings, and bows and arrows.

THINK ABOUT IT

Draw a picture of an Aztec warrior. What clothing or weapons does your warrior have? Now go online to find out what historians think Aztec warriors looked like. How does your picture compare?

Aztec warriors used sharp obsidian in their weapons.

They threw spears using objects called atlatls. They had helmets and wore armor made of thick cloth. Their shields were made of leather or wood. Some of the best warriors were called eagle and jaguar warriors. They got special treatment, costumes, and gifts. They were respected throughout the empire.

After taking control, the Aztec army forced defeated city-states to give tributes to the empire. These were payments of food, clothing, and other goods. In return, the city-states were able to keep their own leaders. The Aztec army did not stay after tributes were collected. The Triple Alliance split tributes. But most of it went to Tenochtitlán. The tributes helped pay for palaces and other

building projects. The conquered city-states also had to send soldiers to all of the empire's future battles. So the Aztec army grew bigger with each city-state it defeated.

15
Age when Aztec boys began training as warriors.

- Aztec warriors were highly trained and skilled.
- Warriors used weapons such as obsidian swords.
- The army made city-states pay tributes to the empire.
- The Aztec army grew bigger and bigger by including captive soldiers.

The Aztecs Had Upper and Lower Classes

Everyone had their place in Aztec society. The emperor ruled over everyone. But each city-state had its own lower and upper class. At the top was the ruler, or *tlatoani* ("chief speaker"). He was the head warrior. He had to lead and win a battle before becoming the ruler.

The *pipiltin* was the class of nobles. Aztecs believed the gods made the nobles to rule over others. The nobles had special rights by birth. They had the best homes, education, clothing, and food. They were warriors, priests, judges, chiefs, and other important people.

A model Aztec village

Most Aztecs belonged to the commoner class, the *macehualtin*. They included farmers, carpenters, stonecutters, craftsmen, and shopkeepers. They served the nobility. Most people of the macehualtin were grouped into a *calpulli*. A calpulli was a neighborhood unit within the

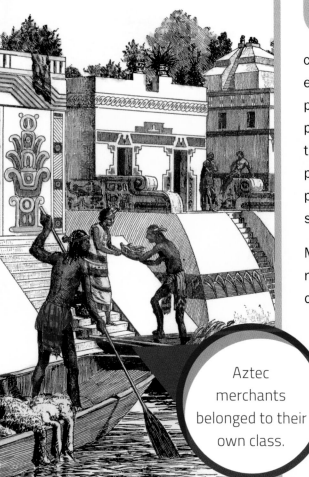

Aztec merchants belonged to their own class.

city-state. An elected headman in each calpulli distributed land to the people. They worked the land and paid tribute from it. Slaves were at the bottom of Aztec society. Some people became slaves in order to pay their debts. Others became slaves as punishment.

Most priests were children of nobles, but they could be from any class. They were servants of the gods. Priests were in charge of temples, festivals, and some schools. Some were warriors or scribes. Others read the stars. And women could be priests as well.

Children Were Stretched Out

Children went through many rituals as they grew up. Aztec children went through stretching ceremonies. Each year, their noses, ears, fingers, and legs were pulled. Aztec parents believed this would make sure their children grew well.

Aztec boys went to the telpochcalli to become warriors.

By the age of four, Aztec children had chores and had to follow rules. They were to obey their elders. They learned to speak softly and eat neatly. They helped prepare home altars for the gods. Sometimes they misbehaved and were punished. Then they might be stuck with thorns. Or they were tied up and forced to sleep outside.

Boys and girls went to school sometime between the ages of 10 and 20 years old. But Aztec parents decided on their child's education much earlier. When children were

SUPER SWEEPERS

Aztec spaces were very tidy. Children learned to use brooms at a young age. Priests swept temples. Women swept their homes and yards each day. But sweeping was not just for cleaning. It was an important ritual. Aztecs believed sweeping would keep the gods happy and the world in order.

4

Age, in days, that children had a bathing and naming ceremony.

- Aztec children went through many rituals as they grew.
- Children would be punished for bad behavior.
- Noble boys and girls attended a temple school called the calmecac.
- Teenage boys trained for military life at the telpochcalli.

just 20 days old, their parents chose which school they would go to during another ceremony. There were two types of schools. One school was the *calmecac.* This temple school trained nobles and some commoners. Boys learned to be priests and other leaders. Girls attended separately and studied religion. Some trained to be priestesses and healers. Many commoner teenage boys went to the *telpochcalli.* They trained to be warriors.

The Aztecs Had Hundreds of Gods

Religion was found in every part of Aztec life. Aztecs believed the earth, sky, and sun all had powers. They believed humans and nature were connected.

The Aztec people had hundreds of powerful gods and goddesses. Ometeotl ("Two God") was the creator of the gods. It was found everywhere, and it was both male and female. Quetzalcoatl ("Feathered Serpent") was the god of wind and learning. Tlaloc ("God of Rain and Lightning") was so important that he was worshipped in the Great Temple in Tenochtitlán. And Aztecs believed Huitzilopochtli ("Hummingbird of the South") guided them to settle in the Valley of Mexico.

Hummingbirds were closely associated with Huitzilopochtli.

NEW FIRE CEREMONY

Every 52 years, the Aztecs waited for the end of the world. They cleaned out their homes. They put out every fire so that all was dark. On a mountain, priests watched the stars in the night sky. The stars showed them that the world would go on. Then they lit a fire on a sacrificed warrior. People lit torches. They ran the new fire to the rest of the empire.

Earlier cultures also built temples to worship Quetzalcoatl.

Aztec origin stories said the gods had sacrificed themselves to make life on earth. The Aztecs needed to repay the gods by offering food, animals, or human blood. This would keep the gods pleased and the world working as it should.

Every month, the Aztecs had big celebrations and ceremonies. Everyone took part. Priests prayed. People danced and lit fires. They offered food, drink, and gifts to the gods. They sacrificed people and animals.

3
Number of souls Aztecs believed one person had.

- The Aztecs believed humans and nature were connected.
- The gods were part of all areas of Aztec life.
- Aztecs repaid the gods through celebrations and sacrifices.

Human Sacrifices Lost Their Hearts

The Aztecs believed sacrifice was necessary. It helped the sun rise, the rain fall, and the crops grow. They needed blood to repay the gods for making the world. So the Aztecs sacrificed their own bodies. Priests pierced their arms, ears, tongues, and other body parts. They offered the blood to the gods. They sacrificed animals such as birds.

The Aztecs also sacrificed other humans. They were not the only ones to do this. People from China to Europe to North America have made human sacrifices.

Each month, there were human sacrifices at temples throughout the Aztec Empire.

Many victims were warriors captured from conquered city-states. But children, men, and women of all ages were sacrificed, too.

Victims were bathed and sometimes painted. They were dressed to look like gods. Often a victim was taken to the top of the temple. A priest would cut into the victim's chest and rip out the beating heart. Then the body was kicked down the steep

The Aztecs made human sacrifices as offerings to the gods.

temple steps. Sometimes, warriors and nobles ate some of the victim's flesh. The flesh was said to have the power of the gods.

When they ran out of victims, the Aztec army used flower wars to supply more. These were small battles fought against other city-states. The Aztec army didn't try to conquer the enemy. They just terrorized them and took a few captives to sacrifice. The flower wars were especially important when there was a shortage of food, as there was in 1450 to 1454. The Aztecs believed the gods were angry and needed more sacrifices.

126
Number of humans whose remains were found at the Great Temple at Tenochtitlán.

- The Aztecs believed sacrifice was needed to repay the gods.
- Priests offered their own blood and animals at temples.
- The Aztecs sacrificed humans during important ceremonies.
- Sacrifice victims could be warriors, men, women, or children.

Many sacrifices happened at temples or pyramids similar to this one.

The Aztecs Were Smart Farmers

Planting and growing were important parts of Aztec daily life. Aztec farmers planted maize (corn), grains, beans, squash, and chilies. They did not have farm animals or plows. They used sticks and hand tools.

The Valley of Mexico has wet and dry seasons. Farmers learned to control water so their crops would grow. They built dams. In swamps, they marked out rectangles. Then they built walls to surround each rectangle. The Aztec farmers

Aztec farmers used canoes to get around.

dumped soil inside these rectangles. The spaces in between the rectangles would fill with water and were wide enough to fit a canoe. These rectangles were called *chinampas*, or floating gardens. In some areas, farmers built short walls across hillsides. This made fields that were flat instead of sloped.

People traded items and services at markets. The city of Tlatelolco held its famous market every day. The crowds could reach 50,000. Cotton cloth and cacao beans were used as money. People could buy ceramics and carvings. They could find baskets, feathers, and jewelry. Wealthy merchants were called the *pochteca*. These merchants traveled to faraway places. But they did more than buy and sell. They also spied,

The remains of the ancient city of Tlatelolco can still be seen today.

fought, and brought back goods. They gathered important news and information, too.

1.5 million

Number of people the Aztec food system supported in the Valley of Mexico.

- Aztec farmers planted many crops.
- Farmers invented ways to control water to make sure their crops grew.
- Tlatelolco was famous for its huge market.

THINK ABOUT IT

Think about the last time you were at the store. How was it similar to the Aztecs' system of trade? How was it different? What about the types of items you could buy?

17

The Aztecs Were Builders and Thinkers

By 1519, Tenochtitlán was one of the largest cities in the world. It was approximately the same size as Paris, one of the largest cities in Europe at the time. When the Spanish arrived, many had likely never seen such a large city.

Rulers lived in palaces with gardens and pools. Nobles lived in palaces or two-story homes. Commoners lived in small homes with adobe walls.

Several commoner homes shared a patio.

In approximately 1449, the emperor Montezuma I ordered a huge dike to be built. This protected homes and fields from floods. Engineers built aqueducts to bring fresh water to the city. People paddled canoes through the canals. They crossed bridges to the mainland.

The empire's largest temple was Tenochtitlán's Templo Mayor, or

Templo Mayor is in ruins today, but it was once the Aztec Empire's largest temple.

200,000

Estimated population of Tenochtitlán in 1519.

- The largest temple was Templo Mayor, or the Great Temple.
- The Aztecs used water technology such as aqueducts and a dike.
- The Aztecs used two calendars.

THE CALENDAR STONE

In 1790, workers found the Calendar Stone. It had been lost and buried for more than 300 years. In the middle was the face of the sun god. People believe this stone was used during human sacrifices. It may have been a special place for hearts, blood, and offerings to the gods.

the Great Temple. Many important rituals took place there. This temple had two pyramids with steps. The Aztecs left offerings to the gods buried deep in the floors and stairways.

Aztec priests and nobles studied the stars. They used the stars to make two calendars. A 260-day calendar helped them

track rituals and tell the future. Each day had a number and a name, such as 11 Jaguar or 3 Rain. The Aztecs also used a 365-day calendar. This tracked the seasons and months.

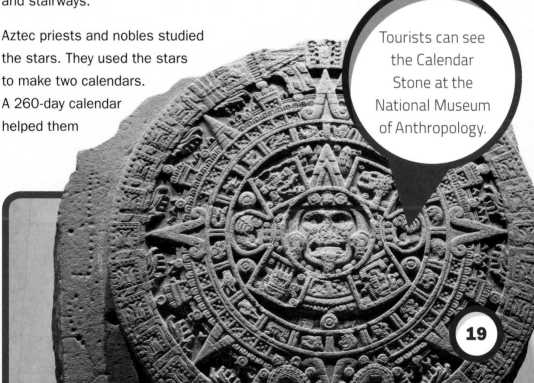

Tourists can see the Calendar Stone at the National Museum of Anthropology.

9

The Aztecs Made Art from Feathers and Stones

The Aztecs made all kinds of art. They made sculptures, paintings, and clay pottery. They wove feathers into beautiful designs. They wrote speeches, prayers, poems, and riddles. The Aztecs believed the best art could communicate with the gods. Art also helped record the history of their people.

Aztec painters made books of pictures to tell stories. This kind of book is called a codex.

A codex was usually made out of long, folded pieces of bark or animal hide. Some stretched more than 46 feet (14 m) long. The books had pictures and symbols, because Aztecs did not have an alphabet or written words.

A codex recorded important information, from rituals to warfare to laws. One famous Aztec codex is called the *Codex Mendoza.* It tells about

The *Codex Borbonicus* was written by Aztec priests.

11

Approximate height, in feet (3.5 m), of the Coatlicue statue.

- Aztecs sometimes used feathers in their art.
- Painters made books of pictures and symbols to tell stories.
- Aztec artists made sculptures using stones, wood, and shells.

sculptures. One of these sculptures was discovered in 1790. It shows the earth goddess Coatlicue ("Lady of the Serpent Skirt"). She has a necklace of hands and a skirt of snakes. The statue now sits at a museum in Mexico City.

Statue of Coatlicue

Aztec daily life, tributes, and rulers. It was made around 1541, after the Spanish came. Afterward, some native people used the alphabet brought by the Spanish to write about their lives in their own language, Nahuatl.

Aztec sculptors carved into stones, wood, and shells. Often they carved gods or animals, such as snakes or jaguars. The Aztecs believed that magical powers lived inside the

The Aztecs Played Games and Made Clothes

The Aztecs enjoyed playing games. The most popular was a fast-paced game known as "the ball game." This game had a court with high walls. Stone rings stood on each side. Players scored by getting a hard, heavy rubber ball through the other team's ring. But players could not use their arms or feet. They had to use their knees, thighs, and hips. The game could cause injury and even death. The ball game was considered good training for warriors. It was played by both commoners and nobles.

Aztecs played a type of board game, too. It was called *patolli*. Players sat at a rubber mat with squares painted on it. Each player had counters colored red or blue. Players moved the counters after throwing dice on the board. Their dice were beans with numbers painted on

The Aztecs played the ball game in courts like this one.

Aztec women wove cloth from agave plants.

6

Size across, in inches (15 cm), of the rubber ball used during Aztec ball games.

- The Aztecs played a type of ball game using only their knees, thighs, and hips.
- Players bet something of value before starting a ball game or a game of patolli.
- Aztec women wove cloth with complicated patterns.

them. The first player to move the counters to the other side of the mat won. The winner would get the loser's jewelry, feathers, or whatever else had been bet.

Women spun and wove cloth in their homes. They crushed plants and insects to make dyes. Aztec women wore long skirts and loose shirts with belts. They wove clothing with complicated patterns. Nobles wore cotton clothing with colorful designs and jewelry. Commoners wore clothing made from agave plant fibers.

The Aztec Empire Fell to the Spanish

In 1519, the Spanish arrived in Tenochtitlán. They were led by Hernán Cortés. The Aztec emperor Montezuma II was suspicious of the strangers. But he welcomed them. The Spanish were amazed at Aztec civilization and wanted its riches for themselves. Cortés took Montezuma prisoner in his own palace. War broke out in 1520. Montezuma was killed. His nephew, Cuauhtemoc, took his place. But the damage was already done. Many Aztecs started dying from diseases brought by Cortés and his men.

Cortés joined forces with local enemies of the Aztec Empire. Some allies came from city-states that had not been conquered by the

European paintings show how they viewed the Aztecs.

THINK ABOUT IT

Imagine you are a local enemy of the Aztec Empire in 1519. Would you join forces with Cortés? Write a paragraph about it.

40

Percent of central Mexico's native population that was killed by a virus called smallpox in one year.

- Led by Hernán Cortés, the Spanish arrived in Tenochtitlán in 1519.
- Many Aztecs died from diseases brought by the Spanish.
- Many native allies aided the Spanish.
- In 1521, Tenochtitlán fell to the Spanish, and the empire ended.

empire. In 1521, the Spanish led a final attack on Tenochtitlán. It lasted almost three months. The Spanish had horses, guns, cannons, and other weapons. But most importantly, the Spanish had gained more than 200,000 native allies. These native allies knew how to cut off the Aztecs' food and water. On August 13, 1521, the Aztec emperor Cuauhtemoc surrendered. The great empire had come to an end.

The Spanish built a new city right on top of Tenochtitlán. They tried to force their religion on the people who lived there. They banned human sacrifice. They drained Lake Texcoco and made many native people work in silver mines. Meanwhile, Spanish ships arrived to settle "New Spain." But the Spanish had taken over only the city-state of Tenochtitlán. The fight to rule over other city-states from the Aztec Empire would continue for a long time.

Still, the Aztec people kept their culture alive. They blended Spanish beliefs of Christianity with their traditional beliefs. They continued to speak Nahuatl, make art, and farm the land for many years.

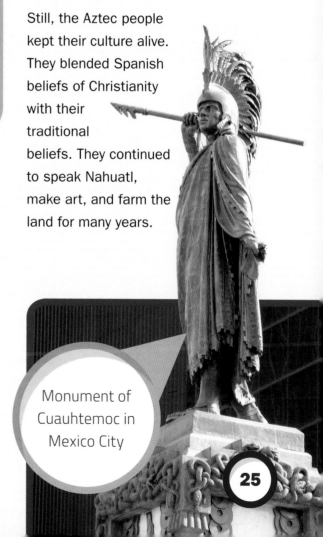

Monument of Cuauhtemoc in Mexico City

Aztec History Lives On

In 1824, a London museum displayed Aztec objects. This helped raise interest in the Aztec world. People have continued to learn about the Aztecs since then. They look at written records left by the Spanish. They study the Aztec traditions that people still practice today. They also study objects and remains from Aztec times.

Aztec mask displayed at the British Museum

Mexico City sits on top of the ruins of Tenochtitlán. In 1978, workers uncovered Templo Mayor. Researchers have studied many other Aztec sites. People have found temples, sculptures, and other pieces of Aztec life. Many of the finds are on display at the National Museum of Anthropology and History in Mexico City. Tourists can view Aztec ruins and other ancient sites.

Spanish and Aztec cultures mixed to form present-day Mexico. Aztec images appear in Mexican writing, music, and art. Today there are more than one million people who speak Nahuatl, the language of the Aztec Empire. People still know old ways of weaving, planting, and more. Many

SPEAKING THE LANGUAGE

English has borrowed several words from the Aztecs' Nahuatl language. *Tomato*, *chocolate*, and *coyote* all come from Nahuatl. Aztec brides and grooms tied parts of their clothing together during their wedding. This practice is found in many other old cultures, too. This ritual is where the phrase "to tie the knot" comes from.

8,000

Number of Aztec objects discovered at Templo Mayor.

- People learn about Aztec life through records, traditions, and discoveries.
- Templo Mayor was discovered in 1978.
- Tourists can visit Aztec ruins and museums.
- Aztec culture is a part of Mexican culture today.

mix Christian religious beliefs with native traditions.

The Aztecs made up the greatest empire in central Mexico. Today, the Aztec Empire remains an important part of Mexican history. People continue to discover more information about this amazing civilization.

Dancers at an Aztec ceremony in Texas show off their costumes.

1325
The Aztecs arrive in what is now Mexico City and found the capital of Tenochtitlán.

1428
Tenochtitlán, Tezcoco, and Tlacopan form the Triple Alliance. This marks the beginning of the Aztec Empire.

1449
Emperor Montezuma I orders the building of a large dike in Tenochtitlán.

1450
A shortage of food causes the Aztec army to fight flower wars. The flower wars let up when the shortage ends four years later.

1470
The Calendar Stone is built approximately during this year.

1519
Spanish explorers led by Hernan Cortés arrive and meet emperor Montezuma II.

1520
War breaks out between the Aztecs and Spanish. Montezuma II is killed.

1521
The city of Tenochtitlán falls to the Spanish and their native allies.

1541
The *Codex Mendoza* is created, showing Aztec life and its rulers.

1790
Workers discover the Calendar Stone and statue of Coatlicue.

1824
A London museum is the first to display Aztec objects.

1978
Excavations begin on Templo Mayor under Mexico City.

Glossary

alliance
An agreement of organizations to work together.

aqueduct
A structure used to carry water to another place.

bustle
To be very busy, hurried.

celebrations
Gatherings or parties to mark important events.

ceremony
A special event that is very formal.

obsidian
A type of volcanic glass.

rituals
Events that are repeated in the same way.

sacrifices
People, animals, or things that are killed or offered to the gods.

scribes
People trained in writing and record-keeping.

temples
Places where people worshipped the gods and made offerings.

traditions
Ideas and beliefs that are passed down from generation to generation.

For More Information

Books

Clint, Marc. *Aztec Warriors*. Minneapolis: Bellwether Media, 2012.

Honders, Christine. *Ancient Aztec Government*. New York: PowerKids Press, 2016.

Roxburgh, Ellis. *The Aztec Empire*. New York: Cavendish Square, 2016.

Visit 12StoryLibrary.com

Scan the code or use your school's login at **12StoryLibrary.com** for recent updates about this topic and a full digital version of this book. Enjoy free access to:

- Digital ebook
- Breaking news updates
- Live content feeds
- Videos, interactive maps, and graphics
- Additional web resources

Note to educators: Visit 12StoryLibrary.com/register to sign up for free premium website access. Enjoy live content plus a full digital version of every 12-Story Library book you own for every student at your school.

Index

About the Author

Laura K. Murray is the Minnesota-based author of more than 40 nonfiction books for children. She enjoys learning about the fascinating lives of ancient peoples and how they compare with our lives today.